AF605033

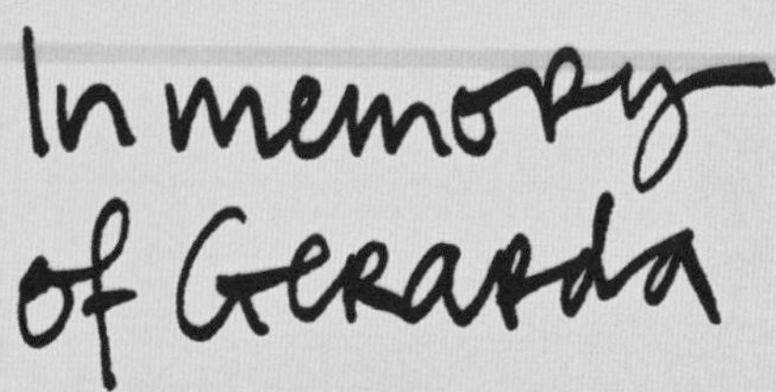

First published in Australia in 2025
by Thames & Hudson Australia
Wurundjeri Country,
132A Gwynne Street
Cremorne, Victoria 3121

First published in the United Kingdom in 2025
by Thames & Hudson Ltd
181a High Holborn
London WC1V 7QX

28 27 26 25 5 4 3 2 1

ISBN 978-1-760-76492-0

A catalogue record for this book is available from the National Library of Australia

British Library Cataloguing-in-Publication Data
A catalogue record for this book is available from the British Library

Front cover: Michel Streich and Sasha Beekman
Design: Michel Streich and Sasha Beekman
Printed and bound in China by C&C Offset Printing Co., Ltd

Thames & Hudson Australia wishes to acknowledge that Aboriginal and Torres Strait Islander peoples are the first storytellers of this nation and the Traditional Custodians of the land on which we live and work. We acknowledge their continuing culture and pay respect to Elders past and present.

gone

michel streich

It happened

on a quiet morning

in autumn.

I woke early and saw that my bird had died during the night.

The bird's body was still there, a silent, feathery shape, but all life had left it.

My fluttering,

chirping,

hopping

bird

was

gone.

I gently carried the body into the garden and dug a little hole.

And there

I buried

my bird.

I was sad,
but that was all right.

It is sad when
a life ends.

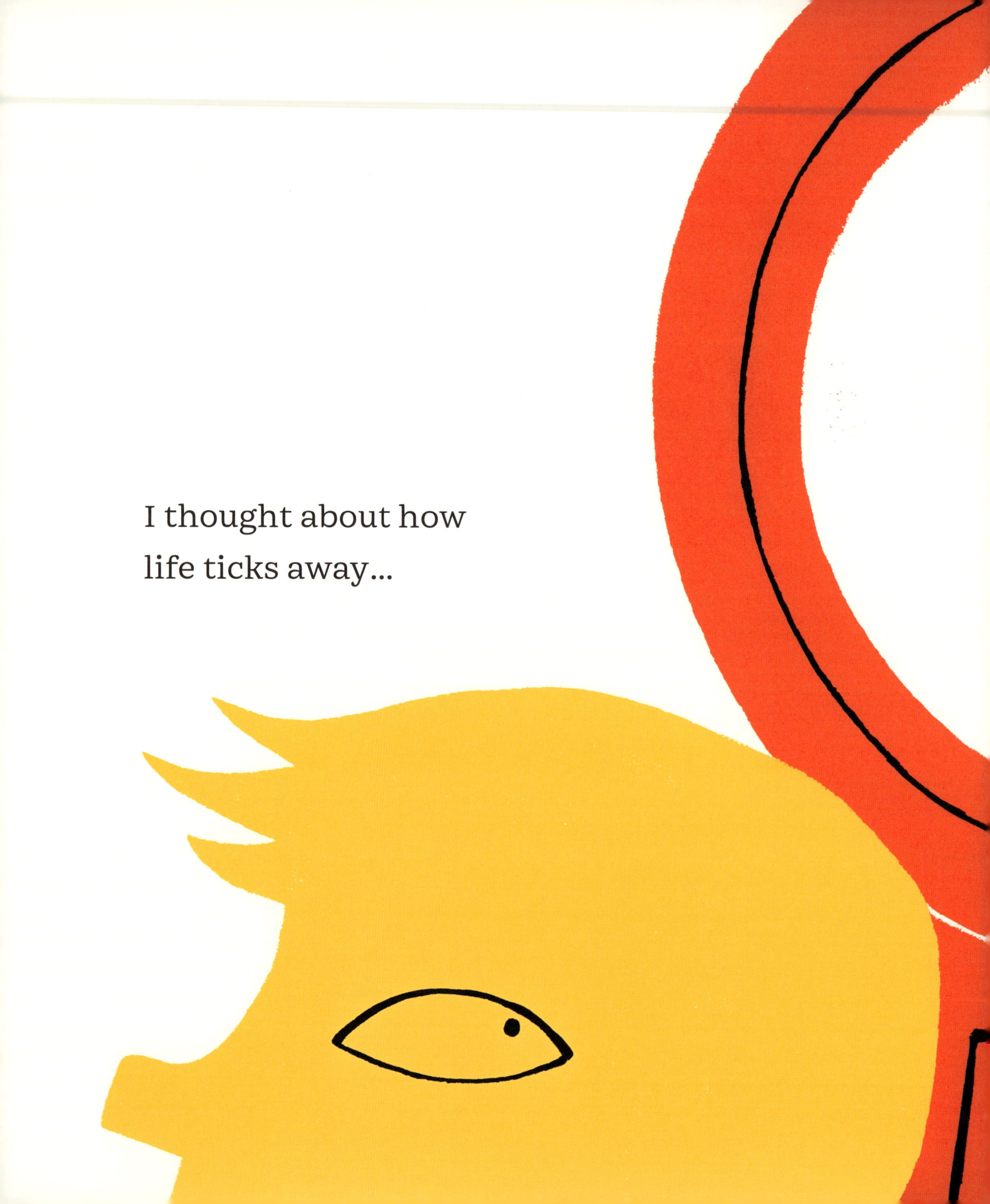

I thought about how
life ticks away...

One minute,
one hour,
one day
at a time.

Some lives are very long. They stretch

over years and years and outlast many things.

Some lives

are very

short.

But where do we go when we die?

My mum says we go to heaven.

My sister thinks we come back in another form, as a child maybe, or as a rabbit or a fish.

Or as a bird!

Grandpa thinks we just stop breathing

and that's it.

We turn into soil

and become part of nature again.

I wasn't sure.

I learned to carry the sadness.

Some days
it was heavy…

And some days it was almost gone.

But my memories stayed with me, always.